THE EIGHTH DAY

ROD JELLEMA

NEW & SELECTED POEMS

DRYAD PRESS

WASHINGTON, DC & SAN FRANCISCO

ACKNOWLEDGEMENTS

Seventeen of these poems appear in print for the first time in this book. *Twenty* other new poems, not published in the author's previous books, first appeared in the following periodicals and anthologies between 1979 and 1984: *Allegheny Magazine, Baltimore Renaissance* (New Poets Series, 1980), *Calvert Review, Garland Editions* (Heatherstone Press, 1981), *Georgia Review, Eighty Poets for the Eighties* (Poetry Now Press, 1983), *Motif, Poet Lore, Poetry Now, The Poet Upstairs* (Washington Writers Publishing House, 1979), *The Reformed Journal, De Strikel, Three Rivers Poetry Journal,* and *West Branch.*

Twenty-eight of these poems have been selected from Rod Jellema's *The Lost Faces* (Dryad Press, 1979) as follows: "Ancestors;" "Chickens;" "Children of Hamelin" (8 parts); "Cutting Paper with Matisse;" "Distances: Christmas 1973;" "Early Coffee;" "Early Morning Exercise, Lake Michigan;" "First Climb up Three Surfers Peak;" "Fishing Over Shipwrecks, I Catch the Word *Spectral*;" "Fresh Fruit for Breakfast;" "A Gruntled Poem for Greeting a Feckful and Wieldy Day;" "Head Down;" "Heading In;" "Holding On;" "Lament;" "Missing Sleep;" "Potatoes;" "Randall Jarrell (1914-1965);" "Reconciliation;" "Report from Near the End of Time and Matter;" "Second Commandment;" "Sidewalk Snowplows: Holland, Michigan in 1940;" "The Shore of the Sky;" "Touching it;" "Two Sleepless Men;" "The Weather is Always Good;" "The Work of Our Hands;" "X."

Thirteen of these poems have been selected from Rod Jellema's *Something Tugging the Line* (Dryad Press, 1974) as follows: "Arm out the Window;" "Because I Never Learned the Names of Flowers;" "Davey Falling;" "Going to Work at Yaddo;" "Incarnation;" "Industrial Park;" "Letter from Home;" "Mrs. Van Den Bosch;" "On Vacation, Teaching Bass;" "Poem Beginning with a Line Memorized at School;" "Seeing Pictures at the Elementary School;" "Sisters, Daughters;" "Walk the Edge."

The writing of this book has been supported by a fellowship from the National Endowment for the Arts (1980), a summer grant from the Creative and Performing Arts Board of the University of Maryland (1982), and residence writing fellowships at Ossabaw Island (1979, 1981) and at Yaddo (1980, 1982). Special thanks also to Myra Sklarew.

This project is partially supported by a grant from the Maryland Arts Council.

Library of Congress Cataloging in Publication Data
Jellema, Rod
    The Eighth Day: New and Selected Poems
        I. Title   II. Title: 8th day.
PS3560.E4654   1984   811'.54   84-40280
ISBN 0-931848-60-1;   0-931848-61-X (pbk.)

DRYAD PRESS
15 Sherman Avenue
Takoma Park, Maryland 20912

P.O. Box 29161 Presidio
San Francisco, California 94123

Son David
Son Michael

a Frisian proverb says,

Ast·it niet sègge kinst
must it mar singe:

If it can't be said
you must sing it.

Contents

III Incarnation

IV Praise Mother Dark

V Concerto for the Left Hand

VI   *Incarnality*

VII   *The Eighth Day*

I

Come Dark

Nightrise from the Observation Deck
of the World Trade Center

Just before lights come on
in the skyscrapers down below
you suddenly see
evening doesn't fall

darkness does not sift down
like black slavic flour.
It rises. From here you can see it
steam off Seventh Avenue

the smoke of horns and cellos
it vents through tunnels and pipes
past windows, it pours
from garrets and unlit rooms,

it is in the valleys
down blouses and shirts, it lurks
under bandages, waits
in cracks, down throats

you can watch through glass up here
as if through waving gills
the changing face of the deep
where nothing had to be at the start

to say *let there be dark*

A Word in the Glare

"Few of the blind are mad," Roethke told his journal—
then wagered his mind by leaping with open eyes
down the shafts of poems into halls of light.
And Edward Hopper took his life to paint
the terrible proportion of light to emptiness,
a final room containing nothing else, and full of it.
What we can't help staring into is not just the invisible
presence of God, but also his visible absence.

This is not an age of dark, but of glare.
The Scriptures warn of it: woe unto them
that put darkness for light, and light for darkness.
Woe to them that deflect us from signs and dreams
to the lighted streets and squares of authorized lives.

These complex pictures force the imagination
back to thing, and back to so simple a thing as a word.
I want now simply to bring in hand the light and dark
of one of the single words for which I grieve: Treblinka.
It makes three winks, a petticoat, tremble of bell
or silver, magic light forever charred like chimneys
stuck in the throat of history: Treblinka.
Though there's not enough dark to show it, I shake the candle
I've lit for a lunatic word I do not want to say: Treblinka.

Two Sleepless Men

If you've ever worked in the building trades,
you know how you almost get used to the hammers
that knock asleep through dust and wind
of hallways as long as night. But just
beneath those beats you feel your fear
of slipping off rafters and thrilling down through ribs.

Maybe long ago some carpenter
new to the trade went back to the job
one night—let's say for his lunchpail—
and found between the studs
nine moons skating in drops of water
over its black enamel—and possibly shadows
of willow dancing through the bonework—
and maybe he joined them—what if he did?—

so maybe that's who's prowling tonight,
keeping you awake: some workman,
not thieving or lost, but back to visit
your long-since settled neighborhood.
Confused by thick and paint and how
the trees have grown, I'm looking for something.
You'll help if you turn out your light.

Sidewalk Snowplows:
Holland, Michigan in 1940

This must have been the last American town
to hire through snow
the shake of bells on the necks of horses.
Good morning began far out in the black
of barns, then lit up and sputtered into town
and jingled up the wind to our waking.
The snow didn't drop from dark or roofs
like the cold of sabbath bells
so much as it turned and rose like flakes
of horsey steam toward windows, ringing crystal.

Sometimes that sound was only the ching of glass
as a milkman struggled across the slippery yards—
but sometimes I could see in the frosty lights
a V-shaped sidewalk plow cut through, could hear
the snorting horse getting proverbed along
in Dutch by its redfaced farmer.
This is back in a time when everyone knew
the war would never come, back when children
were warned they should never give in
and lie down drowsy in blankets of snow.

Missing Sleep

Slow down
sleep is not
the kind of train
you can run for,

remember
a crossing of tracks
with sand and still water
far back.

all your missed trains
set out
the steam and little bells
look for you

the wails and swinging
lights go out
to find you
at the old secret,

that foggy swamp
where there's
a rowboat
a boy you know

and ticking rails
half a mile short
of the boarded-up
hometown station.

Head Down

He disconnects the office intercom,
loosens his tie. His nose
works down the crook in his arm, flannel
sweet with his mother's washday soap,
down winters of corduroy steam
to the face of his sixth-grade teacher.
Drown out the Indian wars, shut off
the flow of exports from Madagascar
and Miss Kooman points her pointer
and says, "Put your head on the desk."

He can make enough dark with his hands
to let the drumbeats in.
Through hemp and chocolate trees
he tracks the star-footed birds
out plains and canyons
scratched through the wood
where no one's allowed to write.
Before he raises again that treaty his face
into old clock-tick and new fluorescent hum,
he swears he will sometime carve his name
against the rules forever
deep in the top of the desk.

Reconciliation

The punishment was always just
to be alone. Its only sentence
was voices through window and floor,
light holding on
till talk ran down with the sky
toward darkness and sleep.

For the life of us
we didn't have words at our house.
Sadness was a door, love
was clean smells, the porch light.
So forgiveness even now
is a trip through night going cool,

engine fumes droning underfoot,
horns, night people I hear
and never see, gravity leaning me right
and then left over sudden pools of streetlight.
It is crunch and ping of gravel under tires,
a farm barking soft and clear, me

drowsing in the night's skin.
I don't want to break it, I only stir soft
against my father's white shirt blurred green
by dashlights to feel his daydream
of lifting a son from damp sheets,
the tight arms of two making both of us

one and half-asleep down steps
and over the grass. Waves nudge our shoreline
awake, but I only come back,
eyes full of light, at the ice cream store:
mica, ice cream, white shirt, star.

Mrs. Van Den Bosch

I was in her dark house next door just once,
and she gave me a cookie. She used to catch rain
in a shiny silver tub; it slid down so clean
I think Mr. Van Den Bosch scrubbed their roof
every week with Dutch cleanser, and waxed it.

I almost never saw her, but she said one day,
while I stood at her rushing downspout after rain,
how soft the water was. I didn't dare to touch.

Mr. Van Den Bosch, our landlord, who kept things straight,
put his plain and dull black bike in our garage
every night. His pants clips stared like giant spectacles,
black handcuffs, under the iron saddle. The bike
stood stiff, never leaned against our wood.

Bending into the splashes of sun and silver that time
I asked her, "why do you save rainwater?"
and she said it made her hair soft.

Her long hair was greying, bunned back
tight, and no one ever went into that house
but me (once) and Mr. Van Den Bosch,
dismounting at 5:35 hunting things to fix.
She stole outside only once in a while for rain.

I would lie in the dark
to think there must be something near
to touch and feel the soft hair.

Davey Falling

On that day the boy shall come down at dusk
from the vacant hill, pulling his battered kite
over the ice-patched road, letting it scrape
and break. Behind the yellow
weeping windows of the kitchen
the soup shall whisper grace.
He shall smell his clean hands
and sit down between small songs his sisters.
Their forks shall chime together to ring the plates.
As easy as the blowing of steam from their cups
shall be the naming of the day's things.
His mother's fingers shall free a slow dance
in his shoulder-bone; his father's words
shall trust like the eyes of his English setter,
shall lay him down to sleep, and he
shall know, years later, always,
at any tugging of a line or string, shall know
that he had almost gotten home.

Sisters, Daughters

My two older sisters went suddenly wide
in the hips, wore bandages called bras,
girdled down flat their bellies and butts.
There was a secretive hush through the house
like a sickly smell, something clamped tight
like their silken knees. I missed the ease
of the rabbits we had been, and
my father started taking me fishing.

You my three daughters, all born dead,
would now be growing round and sweet
and shy. I take your brother fishing.
He leaps through the brush at the shore,
lean and quick as the tip of his flyrod.
He phones his girl every night. I look
at the curved river, missing you.

Holding

We skate out onto thin ice
after nine, but there's concrete
tennis court beneath and floodlights above.
The little kids on wobbly ankles, pushing
their mothers' kitchen chairs, have gone;
the easy high-school crowd is laughing into cars.
Fewer now and alone, we dare to skate
boys with girls. The snow holds its breath.

Through woolen mittens and coats
we feel each other's backs, alive.
We shout and laugh to the dark
while beyond our yellow square of light
the houses of the town going small and orange
are ticking and ticking their clocks.

Arm Out the Window

Arm out the window going cold and white
in the moon, he steers the white lines
through Ohio and other dark states.
A fellow Volvo honks through the black
as though they share a belief
that lowers its pitch as they pass.
Silver leaks out of a barn.
Trucks flash signs like priests
crossing themselves to gravestones.
The summer fading like suntan,
he kicks the dimmer switch and passes
a Mayflower van, its canvas flapping
dew, his right foot quick on the gas.

Walk the Edge

Get over the dunes and start along the shore
at sundown; bring big pockets, walk
not to go but to hoard
the cracks and grainings and lights
in driftwood and stones.

Make the walk spring or fall
when few cottage lights up the dunes
can distract the drift
of your going or coming back. Drift.
Let it be down and into,
not along shore, that you go. Down.
Drift down

inside the spindrift
watch the wet edge for shapes
behind your eyes: fishes; knots.
You can toss most shapes back;
the lake can take its time to finish them:

as deep as you are now
driftwood burns white in the dark
with time for wet sand to rub
the parent stars awake
against bone-touch of branches—
sandtime, slow as the turning of earth.

But that far in is when to turn back.
Now you are almost too far in for love,
almost out of time, turn now quick
to time, take breath to rise up,
you must get back, back up

to some landmark tree on a hill
can point you inland toward towns
and streets small but familiar,
the damp air of your room,
toward raucous morning
when grit of sand in the sheets
and your heavy pockets
are almost strangers.

   (to son John, 1972)

Trout Run
A Poem in Seven Movements

(1) Coming Back in Autumn

Outside the yellow cave my headlights made,
something stirred. But people who know this road
learn to forgive dark things the light can't find;
they'll forgive my ignoring what might have lit up
on the walls of that cave the way they've forgiven
some sad long night of their own when the river
had no stars. Up here in Trout Run, Steam Valley,
they know how light held under ice this time of year
makes little fists that strike far south of here
like cold stars pounding rocks in the river's mouth.

So they learn to let go the light. I also try
to let go. Go gentle, I want to say—but first
my hands and eyes must clench to grasp what it means
to catch: to see, to fix in the mind, to snag
on barbs, to hold a leap as of breath, to stop
the drift of shapes. Well, then, of autumn, of endings,
for dying: all we can string home from the river.

(2) Waking at Clendenins'

In morning light, only the thin
pane of glass can keep the frost
and bloodlit trees on one side,
steam of tea and Verdi on the other.
The mist that ragged the hills at dawn
takes down its flags. Inside,
splinters of red and bronze
drive into the spines of upright books.

There is a way to live
by these exchanges of light:

25

mountains and books in this house
have neighborly words together:
the daughter Lucinda's mythic name
ignites into *Tinda* while Verdi
catches the hues of those leaves,
catches the mathematics of stars.

* * * * * * * * * *

Last night the sky was all the sound
there was. Its tone was dark.
The owl forgot to take in his black sails
so hawks and other minds, red and brash
old hunters, were waiting in blinds.
I woke to a change in key out there,
muted like the front-room window glass
turning bluer each fall toward snow.

I thought the sound might be
the feet of deer who steal down
to the lawn and step onto moonlight,
or stones being rubbed in the stream
or stars in trees. But nothing unhuman
trembles like that. Beyond dry leaves
are whispers, old lovers, old names.

I know last summer's shade trees wait
in cold with their long, meat-eating roots.

(3)   Stranger in the Village

Walking, they say in this house, is good: it smokes the scotch.
I walk the streets of Trout Run in the lurid disguise
of the Stranger. A schoolboy on a bike rides next to me
and asks where I'm going. O just walking, I say,
just walking all over the streets of this old town.
He does not believe me. So now I have him:
now whatever truth I say off-hand will be to him

some flash of legend. He asks me where I'm from.
I shrug. From fairly far away, I say; just came in
from Michigan—and I hook my thumb over the mountains, west.
He winks and grins as though I've told him Pluto.
Now we are friends. How far are you going?
O just to the end of some final street, then back—

and now like a boy encountering some mad Jesus
but trusting, he suddenly stops his weaving bike.
Who are you? he asks. That question older than fire
for which I am never ready. To what can I witness?
I am the piper without a pipe, Adam looking for home—
all this truth tricks me to say I'm a poet—as though
that's still a job. And then the boy reaches back
for some tribal voice as old at least as his mountains.
He hooks his thumb toward the end of the street.
At the hotel, he says, they'd probably give you a beer, for free.

(4)   The Loving Shape of Disorder

It's the kind of afternoon
you'd like to nap in the attic
drowsing under the shuffle and knock of wind.
But we three walk instead
to Bryan Rudge's farm
just up the little road along the stream
where chairs and fruitjars sing like Methodists.
At eighty-five he holds and clips
a formal garden on a shelf, part way up
John's mountain, above the line of the roof.
Bushes and trees are clipped to be
Italian fountains, pairs of lanterns;
everything tries old clapping of hands
to say with art, *remember we are here.*
Darker down in his yard where he legends himself,
two ice-cream-cone trees stand stiff,
circled with painted bowling pins.
From the front window-sill a radio

saws its lock-step rhythm over the wind.
Dark is on the way, and snow,
and Bryan Rudge, who trims out every word
and can name us every track and plant
the length of Steam Valley and up,
probably thinks he works alone
at taming the mountain and carving the human in.
But the shaping of Eden is out of control.
In a spray-painted bush that still hints of fire,
hubcaps hang from plastic fishing line.
Coming back down, two of us talk of primitive art
while one half-remembers a garden he left long ago.

(5)   The Winter I Didn't Come Up

A good cold morning
has the startled eye of a bird.
Cold sings tunes to bones,
somebody said, and I know
the cells in your bones
are out of control and even
the singing by now must ache.
I clap the bird away
and wish you a day when that riot
of cells will ring and beat
and pull and swing like bells
so hard the day will forget to turn
while you listen like a child
for the end and you nod away
to night inside the ringing.

(6)   Last Spring

When I was a child, I knew one thing
for sure: I knew what glory meant:
glory was the dance of bits of dust
in a beam of sunlight pointing to our rug.

John, your good eye gone, you make the bad eye
good, or make it do. You sharpen another sight
past sight, a mind out there in the violet dark
of empty space with which you watch the dance of dust.

The only thing you'd wave a placard for, you said,
was benevolent anarchy. Trying your sight,
I watch that anarchy. It opens and shuts
like chickory, not like a fist. It's spring.

While light comes pointing to lights
the flowers have banked all winter long
birdsong falls out of trees
and again the dew has stained our pantlegs

high up the thighs while we wade a morning
and talk of what the proper work should be
in a point-on-the-map named Buttonwood, PA:
Stitching. Tinkering. Bottling nut-brown ale.

John, last spring is three days past.

(7)   Autumn was Home

There's trouble in the valley
but it's only the world's,
nothing we or the village can fix,
trouble as old as knife or moon.
If sticks and stones tell tales on us,
the tales are only remote—
like what astronomers tell on stars.

My eye stays home. In this old house
two friends weave life and thought
by what they call "collecting a quiet center."
The roads by which they came
slowly die behind, under leaves.
Leafstorms—a favorite word in this word-drunk house—
smother Trout Run like the river in blazes

29

of fractured lights. The dream we walk in
always drifts out of control in its dreamy way.
So almost certainly this legend, this place
we shape will fall again, run off some night
with those reckless boys the lights
of neighboring towns that come riding down
to shoot up the streets of Trout Run in our sleep.

But it is never time to fly.
Plotinus is wrong: the material world is not
a sinking, a failure of wing. It's home.
Night and snow are what happens
to unify the world (we name the rhythm death)
before the boozy birds out there
can start it up again, its holy clamor,

darkness made us talk with harder words,
pain is how the stones catch hold
of the harmony of stars
and maybe it is enough
to have caught the catch of light
all we could string
home from the river.

    (for John and Helen Clendenin)

II

Poems for the Left Hand

Seeing Pictures at the Elementary School

See
four yellow squash
waxing huge and plump
in the grass. Will they explode?
Grinning bees have lit the light green fuse.
The grass is dark. Juanita. Grade 2.

John's castle.
The drawbridge stretches asleep
over a moat of blue
where sailboats bob.
A smudge of black cannon aims at my face.
For all the flags and open doors
there is no road.

See the crooked lumpy dog
bark wide at the doghouse
because the doghouse growls
a rough purple *NO*
where a dog's name should be.
Roger, grade 3. See Roger bark.

My mind can't hear me talking this way.
This is not about art.
My mind is certain the lion is mean,

But Donna's lion gazes
through gauze of black
that drapes the bars
and the caption says,
the lion is mean
because the children have closed the curtain.

Children of Hamelin

Before He Heard of Hamelin

When feet walk the dark street
at night, that's a message
I try to hear. Or I watch
light happen
to startle the hair
of a child or a field of waves.
Sometimes news comes slower,
the swell of bread in the oven,

but either way, a slow and rising flight
or else the splinter
of thin in the wind
is why I flute.

Also because it wasn't just a dream
that I flew once
up from an afternoon nap
up sharp new light where I swung
from the railings and then let go
high up the hole

The steps were running down
like scales below me.
In the hard square kitchen
I promised never again
to fly, but lied.

All trills and tootles now
I travel light. I patch my flappy
sleeves to taste like the smoke
of seasons: today tastes green,

tra-la. I can charm the very
squeaks and thrashings behind the walls
into space that's still.

The next town, Hamelin,
I never heard of. It calls.
Don't call me back.
Or call me,
I like the sound of the wind.

Overheard About Mr. Bunting

(several children of Hamelin speak:)

The rags he flies from his coat
are a torn-up flag.
I don't know what country. It's old.

The first time
I wanted to run
under my bed.
I had forgotten sizes.

The only thing I remember like this
is hearing it whispered long ago
that my father's back-ache came from sleeping in trees.

I dreamt the bridge fell in
and we were like fish
who watched, surprised,
and I thought about Mr. Bunting.

Well, he was anyway
all make-believe
so I ran to him .
and when I got there
he was there.

If my mother saw him at night
she would tell him to turn down the lights.

Every patch
in his coat
is a lit-up place
across a river.

Coming Back Down to Hamelin

*(June 20, 1284: having drowned the rats,
he has been thrown out without pay as a
drunken sorcerer, but now he decides to return.)*

Who could be angry up here?
This path spills happy
drunk in stoney streams
cold and blue to my feet.
The rain or the wine is melting
the mountain, rocks up here
go round to boulders. Faces
can change. These hums in my head
and Saint Francis talking to birds
and my pipe are for people to catch.
So forgive them. Corkscrew back
to the road, uncertain why,
down to that crooked town
and make it dance.

Windy Night in Hamelin

(The Pied Piper speaks:)

To children I'm glow coals of wool
or a tall glass of milk in moonlight,
it depends on the weather.
From one of their houses
a door knob rises over a bush and shines;
my patched coat is cathedral windows,
dogs no longer bark at me.
God bless the air!
The wrinkled colors it shakes.

The cloth merchant's son
has his father's eyes that steal
and I want to bring
strong dark grain from the mountains
but the lights at their table are bright.
That dark woman who hobbles
knocking her cane at a cat
used to stretch out in grass.
I step around the space

of a boy who died.
In my town, if you kicked a flower
you had to pay a just fine.
I kick these clowning leaves
that scratch like sparks and goodbyes,
shuffle a rising dance—
then wonder where the wind goes.
My children you are flying out
and I am trying to follow.

The Notes He Left

Hamelin
June 26
Year of Our Lord 1284
Sunrise   no breeze

The question is not silver
but what's in the air.

Somedays the wind will whine
around corners and windows, restless.

When there are no breaths in the air
you try to hear them.

The rats that sank—were they
the souls of the parents?

I have heard of such things.

Near the end of stillness, there's always
this light whistle through grass

before the rustling
of leaves and wings

and I know that sharp note which the breaths
blow over the hole in the world.

The Hamelin Epilogue

(1)

Hamelin Decree

That the gate through which they passed shall bear a plaque,
As shall the Calvary Mountain which swallowed them.
That the story shall be painted in windows and churches.

That after the date set down of the year of Our Lord
All public documents of the town shall add
The date of the year of the going-forth of the children
Thus: *Anno liberorum suorum exitus.*

That no drum, pipe, or musical instrument
Of any kind shall henceforth sound in the street
Leading to the gate through which they passed.
That no tavern be there, nor any joy.

(2)

Needing a Better Word

(1286: a citizen of Hamelin writes:)

Anno Secundo liberorum suorum exitus.

Children is cold and hollow, a lamentation
of ice and wind. The sound is reprimand,
chapped skin, collisions muffled in snow.

Maybe we should call them *startles.*
A *girl* is not as bright as a *flicka*;
chil and *dren* miss all but darkness and bone.

39

I need some winking word for my own young—
but six of my startles sleep in the ground
stubbornly *children* no matter how I call them

and call them, and winter coming on.

(3)

The Piper Still

. . . a world they can live in.

Not here,
these biting needles of light.
Like any old ghost
I refract to silence
bend down easy
to cracks between keys. And I wait.

Because I Never Learned the Names of Flowers

it is moonlight and white where
I slink away from my cat-quiet blue rubber truck
and motion myself to back it up to your ear.
I peel back the doors of the van and begin
to hushload into your sleep
the whole damn botanical cargo of Spring.

Sleeper, I whisk you
Trivia and Illium, Sweet Peristalsis, Flowering Delirium.

Sprigs of Purple Persiflage and Lovers' Leap, slips
of Hysteria stick in my hair. I gather clumps of Timex,
handfuls of Buttertongues, Belly buttons, and Bluelets.

I come with Trailing Nebula, I come with Late-Blooming
Paradox, with Creeping Pyromania, Pink Apoplex,
and Climbing Solar Plexis,

whispering: Needlenose,
Juice Cup, Godstem, Nexus, Sex-us, Condominium.

Industrial Park

All this green hedging
going on: conduits snap and buzz
underneath
and a cable just misses the goldfish
on its way to Plasticore, Inc.
Phoneline nerves sneak along roots
somewhere near the cutworms.

Pressure and voltage climb the network veins
and cascade up at the level of songbirds
into white pavilions with popsicle windows
and tea-wafer roofs. Thousands stream in
through the turnstiles five days a week
to play, unwind, brief and debrief, eat lunch
industriously in the park on spreading music and carpet.
They touch the shiny equipment.

This is miles on the right side of the tracks
where packaged freight slips in and out at night like love
in long and glistening trucks.

So now and then I circle the Capital Beltway round
and round in the blue rubber truck,
dart into those parks from the night like a spark
and drop off under the stars and trees with love
            large oily gear wheels, hard maple sawdust,
            trainmen's lanterns, steam lunch-whistles—
and for use on alternate days
            rolls of pink tickets, striped picnic cloths,
            balloons and streamers, lemonade stands.

Wire Triangulations

In the second layer of the city they called "New York"
almost no objects survived intact
but our teams did find in white ashes
more than twelve million triangular wire sculptures
each with a curved hook protruding from its apex.
These shapes were almost certainly objects of worship:
most are found in small dark windowless rooms
to which is often applied a derivative of their verb
to close, meaning to end, and also of their word for intimate.

We do not yet know just why these protected
and almost indestructible wire triangulations
were so numerous among the occupants of the World
that Killed Itself, or just how they link to the violent
fascination these people had with destruction and death.
The precise meaning and function of these probable gods
will surely be found in our investigation
into the meaning of triads in their religion and into *hanger*—
a word for which our computers will surely uncover a verb.

After Looking Long at His Pictures of the Civil War, Having First Dropped a Chocolate Peanut Butter Pie Upside Down on His Georgia Carpet, I Dream of Zimmer

Water is brown and yellow-brown smoke lies low
in marsh grass. Inhaling. There goes I think
my Uncle Ben with those other baggy soldiers
trudging through sepia brown. Horses tug at caissons
and soldiers slog. They wave to the camera that's taking
these blown-up moving 3-D pictures of World War I
and I totter on the edge of the frames and feel the suck

dizzy until I fall in. I rise, march with a group, fall
in step or try to fall in step, skip to adjust,
use the soldier on my left for a pacer—
but he gets tangled down, stumbles, skips-to-
adjust but trips and hesitates (*yer left, yer left*)
and looks at me for help and it is Zimmer!
We laugh. As backpacks slip and clunk and splat
we hug, then limp off in broken step with each other.
What place is this, I ask, what regiment, which war?

"The peasants have plenty for supper," Zimmer says.
He squints ahead. "We are the klutzes of World War I,
the Losers, hand-picked by the Army for Zeppelin school."
Knowingly we laugh again hard, we hoot and hitch the muddy
tackle up and keep sloshing ahead. Left-footed rookies
in a lost battalion, headed not at all toward
any front, we wade through 1918 happily
toward unsuccess and our era, our distant births,
sensing how baffled those shy girls our mothers will be.

On Vacation, Teaching Bass

Listen, Bass,

Where is your self-respect?
I stood at your pond the last two dawns
under a dissonance of birds doing their bird-thing,
and I did my teacher-poet-at-leisure-thing, my fisherman-thing,
but you weren't doing your bass-thing at all.

I don't mind not existing; I understand about that;
I'm like anti-matter poking in, or God. Okay.
But the colors and whirrs that I pulled
through your world on transparent lines
were images, meant to *do* something, programmed
through your genes for millions of years.

Look. When you see that wounded wobble of red and white stripes
that I call a Daredevil lure, you're supposed to lunge
and strike—or at least get curious and follow.
But on casts and retrieves with just the right flash, vibration,
and turning, I could see down there some thirty of you
shrug in your fishy way without the slightest shock of recognition.

Wake up! Have you no collective unconscious?
Take my Mepps Aglia #2 Spinner (which none of you did take):
it was assaulting two of your senses at once (along with your dreams),

it was 'the feel and body of the awareness that it presents'—
and there you stood, slowly waving pectoral fins
as though you were trying to think, like pre-engineers.
A lure should not mean, but be!
The three of you dullards I did catch
went for fat, stock-response, mere-prosey worms.

One more thing. When I set my hook and get you on the line,
don't just go limp and come up unastonished.
You're supposed to seize the image and run with the line, tug
(I keep the drag on my reel set light; you can probably hear it sing),
run hard, break the skin between our two worlds, twist and shimmy
in air, then arc and dive down deep. Keep tugging!
That's your natural response, you instinct!

Next time we will talk about fly-casting,
maddening colors like stars on the top of your world.
Try to get yourselves open.

Bass dismissed.

III

Incarnation

Application

What is your permanent address?

The wind through Thick Street
hasn't settled down

look for me in words like *startle, plum.*
They may have to forward you back to *dark*

unless I hit the blue and lonely town
whose little lights I almost glimpse
whenever somebody blesses me when I sneeze.

What memberships do you have?

I belong to those who remember
and seldom say
who don't join up with much.

Member. I think I'm a carpal
just left of the spike
in the left hand of Jesus.

Briefly describe the obstacles to your work:

Eve.
No left turn.
That God made sweet sunfish
so full of bones.
Forgetting.
Remembering
it isn't Eve.

Describe the audience you wish to reach with this project.

Far off
in yellow kitchens after supper
they wonder if it's the trees
in the wind or the wind in the trees
and they are really listening for stones.

What other means of support do you have?

    The stick.
    Forgiveness.

    The speech of any child
    who rejects its dying out

    any star out there that lights on straw
    instead of pointing only
    yet another other star out there.

When do you expect to finish?

    Perhaps at hearing my name
    just when I know I no longer need
    that saddest of words, the word *because*

    perhaps some warm afternoon
    between the rise of a sailing breeze
    and the far ring of a phone
    smell of apples halfway up
    a thought about my hand.

Second Commandment

Our church elders pinched a narrow view
of the sin of making graven images.
But the weather, loose catholic wench,
went right on making through the town
her shapes and traces of God.
I saw it sometimes in storms. Wet streets.

My protestant uncle Lyman took a chance:
from spaces behind his eyes he painted
my dead pioneer great-grandmother looking down
so we kids would know how real and kind
and rough and tender the angels look.
And then he made trees, and lights, and other faces.

The skate key under my shirt swung free
like the crucifix of some Irish tough
from the city thirty miles away
as gently the elders were graven one by one.

Incarnation

Coming home through snow, I think the grey face
of my father, little physician, knew cells. Faces.
Loved most his alcoholic patients, tender
toward their long thirst for a home
that denies our only home.

Addiction, he said, is 80-100 proof
that spirit is,
craves to be flesh.
He understood about incarnation.

But my father still had the dazed Galilean
fisherman's habit of looking up.
His eyes pleaded with red cancer to hurry
as though it were a skyriding pillar of fire,

but it was cancer flowering down in the flesh,
and down in grey cells under skull-bone,
in an old synapse, is where God the Father
was speaking Dutch to a child
when my father said *tot ziens* and died.

(*Tot ziens:* "until we see."
Never mind *wiedersehen*, seeing again,
that German illusion. God and the Dutch tongue
know we have never seen much.)

Home. Make the second sandwich while eating the first,
the third while eating the second.
At seven p.m. there is light enough
at the open refrigerator.
Reach into the light for milk, drink it
from the wax lips of the carton. Rinse
the knife. Now tilt the lamp. Spend
the evening reading the morning paper.

But the sky out there will have to be more
than a capsule under a tooth
hissing blue and then black in God's throat.
My furnace burns blue, rattles death
down the hall that goes nowhere but out, out
across snowfield city and faces,
the making of tracks across morning papers.

Christ resurrected as nigger or honky,
broken and waiting for what,
something has to stop this news from becoming home,
these burnings, body counts, thrusts
of needles and rockets into fleshless non-worlds.

How god damned whited and cold
like a sheet of paper I am now,
making tracks, thinking the lines of faces
at the bars, each face as sharply its own
as the labels on bottles that reverse the mirrors,
imprinting the only news for now.

Face by false ascent by phrase
by face by riot I learn, learn that words matter
like bodies, learn not to look up
for some pure-spirit godkin
Christ but down the lost faces
the Word became
before we made it mere word again,
mere tracks in the snow.

Poem Beginning With a Line Memorized at School

Whither, indeed, *midst falling dew,*
Whither, Miss Pfisterer, black-dressed and balding
Teacher of English, lover of Bryant,
Whither did we all pursue
While glow the heavens with the last somethingsomething?

Bradley Lewis, I mean:
Who put aside with his cello and his brushes
Our lusty masculine sneers at his graceful ways,
Skipped the civics exam to father a son
And now designs engines with Mozart turned up loud.

Kenny Kruiter, I mean:
Expelled from high school for incantation with wine,
Who bends the knee to his common daily bread,
Hacks every day at bleeding sides of beef
And cheers twice a week the college basketball team.

Michael Slochak, I mean:
He always stuttered every dull thing he knew
And walked home alone—past home, to one gold period
When, crimson phrase against the darkly sky,
His jet purred into a green Korean hill.

A Gruntled Poem for Greeting
A Feckful and Wieldy Day

All things are down and doing
so commonly green and quick
that I give this clement day
my swerving love.
I sniff and watch in dogged ease
gainly girls at the corner bus-stop
so fretless and seemly
they could be gathering to pluck
dulcet grapes from slopes.
Of all the unmitigated sweet!

This old boyhandled world
picks me down
to such a perfect flation
that I can't uncorporate.
I drag my formity
amuck this alloyed happiness.
Hand me, villain!
my mind is coming hinged.
With bending determination
I earth my old flesh of contention

and shuffle soft-shoed into death
with all deliberate torpor.

The Work of Our Hands

He would come home tired at night from making things,
his hands still dreaming the prints of handles:
my *pakke*, great-grandfather, maker of windmills
                 in Friesland.

Out of the wind, he would probably stare at his fire.
The work could go on alone, sails and beams
angled to translate every pull and push of wind
to the balance of brake-wheel.
While hand-cut spur gears rhyme the shaft,

his shapes could turn in drowsy in his head.
Only the hands remember a good day's work:
it's like falling asleep with your bride,
or fishing in the dark after the fish have stopped
but you think you feel them still through the hand.

I know that space. Though my *pakke* died before I was born,
carving ornate ballustrades in Chicago mansions,
I finally fished and nailed and felt the wind and bought
a sail and now I know that throb in my hand.

The gift is tension, drag. I'll never wish again
to feel the sail rise up from the water and soar
toward the thrill and loop of a hollow scream:
even birds when they sing grip their hands down hard
into bark that is rooted and cuts the wind.

My hands hug shape. The prow leaps down for more.
Pakke, I write and sail as a displaced, unemployed millwright.

(for William Harry Jellema)

Heading In

Night breeze stirs the hair on my arm.
I hear trees moving along the shore.
The mast of my little boat
plots arcs and points in the dark,
uncertain. She bobs no light.

Son John and I all day have reaped the wind
and made the daggerboard tick
as we cut through sunlight and breakers.
His hands are quick to tiller and line.

White stars bloom soft down this desert of water.
Only my hands remember the day.
Each slow flap of sail is an ache in the arms.
I wish all boats had still a man's work,
could bring something back.

I am not quite lost in these reflections of stars.
Pakke's old cells call through my bones
to say, "you are losing your son,'
but a neighbor's light on the dune points home.

Some night as he sails here alone
my son will pick up and bring back
senses the mind can never know about wind,
his past, work, losses, his hands.

(fragment, 1972)

IV

Praise Mother Dark

Early Coffee

Hair and nails grow in the dark;
all night the spiders spin
lines to catch the blue buzz,
pulsing, hum of words
through cells that sleep.
To drowse before dawn is to net
the spin and stretch of things
that darkly grow
as the world tips and falls to light.

The sky has torn its hangnail red.
Through bark and twist of twigs
the morning moves like a herd of steer,
rising stiff from roads. It steams.
Cars begin to stream the freeways,
wide-eyed yellow current down wires.
In breaking light I try to hold
the dark nest that's cupped in my hands.

Fishing over Shipwrecks,
I Catch the Word Spectral

Bells of lost ships
ting as they graze
dark valleys of seaweed.
They follow each other
down the distance of rust,
wait to be heard.

I touch that world deep
with a tremble of thin
fishing line.
Their blind towns wait
for the holds to break.
Learn to let go.

Down there they see line
off the reel of a star
slanting through water.
It ignites the spectral
scales of a fish.
Look up and stay down.

The red of my lure
once waited in black.
Then it scratched
through its fur
and started to glow.
Praise mother dark.

Report from Near the End of Time and Matter

"If only we could see for a moment
the holy light we pursue. . . ."
    —Plotinus

Say it is now the third month of light.
Your eyes can't filter it out. Try
to tuck your head under your blazing arm,
try to find the sloping back to shade.
Out along the flat plane of your gaze
no aura from tree can print itself on your eye.
Remember colors? Thick and cool. Old saints
in glassy rag and skin who hung
between us and the Sunday sun. But now
nothing shines in this total bright.
There is no shadow flickering in a window,
no dark in which to remember depth. Even
the blood shade of your eye-lid is clearing to white.

Lament

I want back
my rib

its old space
whispers
to my cage

pacing
the dark.

Chickens

They stagger off balance, hugging
wings that won't fly. Air
is a stranger's hand to their feathers.
Lidless eyes stuck open,
they reel in and out
earth-tight and cockeyed
through lights that won't go out
till wind is the only dark they know.
Broody for all their dead eggs,
they prawk and gargle dry
through stones, scratch down yards
and yards of the earth.
All night in the brooders, electric
nightmare eggs glare down.
Inside the plastic meat
pumping steroids glow like dying
stars, shoot through entrails
that have nothing portentous to say.

If they could only breed and brood
in some dark
sensing shadows
and what to drift back to
they'd know again to fly
their folded arms.
I throw the dumbclucks some skins
from their scuppernong vine
they cannot fly or climb
and decide I'll fox in some night.
In a wicker basket I'll gather
their lightbulbs, pour scuppernong
wine in their mash,
and the next morning pluck them
from swaying and singing
high in live oaks.

Potatoes

*". . . the scarcely innocent underground
stem of one of a tribe set aside for evil."*
(Ruskin)

The tribe is deadly nightshade,
"used to relax eye muscles" and
to kill. Akin to the bittersweet
we used to strip and hang by its feet
in the dark basement
until it cracked its yellow lids
and wrinkled open red.

Potatoes yawn in that dark. Pale wet
sprouts spill out of eyes
as though the dark had sprung a leak.
Once I secretly shoveled into the furnace
my father's boot, bulging with their stems.
They'll crawl all night blue-veined
toward stairs, toward us.

Cut out their starry eyes
and fling them into black, each one
will beam a limp and stemming eye
back toward light—not to break free
but to blink and catch
the old rhythms that pump potatoes,
innards hugely white in the dark—

feeding 400 years of history,
steaming hills, enough to feed an army.

Lake Michigan Sand Cherries

Good children know that anything bitter
is wrong—so we knew the squat
dark plants on the beach were poison.
But within those rims of white sand bowls
the fruits shone so olive-blackly,
low in the wind, that I once broke through

with my right incisor tooth and my sister
said I would die but I didn't
even get sick or struck from behind
by God or lightning the way you would
if you were at a roadhouse dance
downshore at Saugatuck, say
(that's on the way to Chicago)—

so I forgot about them. They had lost
their Dutch theological sting.
We might as well have called them *beach plums*
the way I hear the rich resorters do
at Cape Cod. We called them nothing at all.

But there's a whirl of a woman comes down
from a hundred miles upshore
where the wind keeps you loving the earth,
and she takes them like notes in a yellow scarf
with an ease I could almost sing about.
I look at this dark-ruby red she has picked

and preserved and sent me in glass,
labeled *sand cherry / 8-82*. I taste
its dangerous lilt toward a dance
for the month of my brith, the wild tang
the Indians call Black Cherry Moon,
and I pray that all her steps
may continue to wink such graces.

The Shore of the Sky

Sleep with me on the beach.
Our sails will flap back and forth
and touch so lightly
we do not feel water
lapping the ribs of the
one washed-out hull we become.
Inside it a red lantern rubs
and slowly swings.
Shooting stars fall down
the tunnels behind our eyes
and hold their matches
still enough
to light up colored birds
and fish on the walls.
We keep waking up
less awake each time
but wide alive to the sky:
we peer up from this long
low field of stargrains
into handfuls of
beach sand hanging high.

Flieger's Barn

Inside the hot green smolder
of unripe straw, the *ching*
of the scythe waits under rust.
In its dark chapel the bell
of the summer cow is still
but it summons anyway the rising
steam from a pail of milk
sweaters of high school girls
heave and fall of lamps
that sway under storms
and startle wings and dust
high up the hoots of rafters.

Red mouth of a woman is what
the poem was moving toward
when it started out,
and butter pressing through
the seams like light—
but it forgot to invent
a road going back.
By now dark owns the barn
but rents it out some nights
to the moon. Inside and out
the red barn beats and flags
from the far-off snow.

Some Aches are Good

Each winter I mislay the summer, but last Christmas day
beach sand shone bright through the dark of a drawer.

Up close a star is not points, it's a stone in a stream,
her hip, light circling like the memory of a hat.

The whores back home were on Commerce Street and their sheets
were gathered in and washed by the Sunshine Laundry.

Some aches are good: green plums, lifting a scab on a knee,
stretching a sprained ankle far down the bed in the morning.

I almost remember hunching in dark at a shore
before my father came with a light to find me.

Ancestors

Their bloodlines curl in fur
far down the cells. At night
they stir, try to peer out
the slit in your eyes.

Softly they tip things
and quick as a cat you wake
to distortions and see
why Picasso painted at night.

Randall Jarrell (1914-1965)

Our legs go limp, will not
lift foot to brake
as he swims up the path of headlights.
Like pain he leaps from darkness,
"and we call it wisdom. It is pain."

These skidmarks are only an afterthought
swerve. Our brights attracted him,
our eyes lost the edge:
we failed to warn him
in the dreams he had of us.

Listening to Comrade Shostakovitch
on the Day of his Death

With eyes closed we can hear
the getting light: bright coats
that flow through the market,
the stun of blue haze
lifting off smoking wheatfields
outside Leningrad.

And still the bass-clef mole.
Deep where we dream
and remember, he cannot find
the moon he's looking for.
Listen: he tracks from
stone to stone, subverting
the earth to chart the landscape
we follow into next
the dark side of the lawn.

V

Concerto for the Left Hand

Cutting Paper with Matisse

Drawing with his scissors, one whole movement
linking "line with color, contour with surface,"
Henri Matisse must have left an awful clutter.
To find those scraps of color now
from which he lifted shapes would be to find
strange negatives of paintings,
the stencils of the firmament.
Perhaps it only happened while cleaning up
that he picked scraps off the floor
and pasted them onto their positives
like pieces of the mirrors
in which his mind was learning to see.
The eyes can never see enough.
He cut his random way through stacks of paper,
even sailed to Polynesia just to study
"the altered proportions of light and space."

This random poem of mine has nothing to study at all;
it follows a child's left hand
strolling a right-handed scissors
through silent planes of snow
to anything. To the stiff paper snowflakes
I tried one day to cut in my room after school,
all geometric, little chops and snips.
To the magnified snowflakes I studied later,
swirling valleys. Through bigger microscopes
I saw fields rinsed by stains of gentian violet
to colors blazing in from every side
and still those shapes, and other shapes that
the dreamer hand remembers and remakes

until the sea is churning spirochetes
and fossil-leaves, tiny birdwings from back
so far behind the lens that only the hand can find them,
and moons, and the sky holds still to show
protozoa orbiting the little bones of fish.

(*Matisse: The Cut-outs.* National
Gallery of Art, October, 1977)

77

Four Voices Ending on Some Lines from Old Jazz Records

(1)   *any little woman*

The red neon sign
makes jumps like knuckles
and I almost forget how blood
moves soft inside.
Hearing it now, the beat,

I don't care a dime
how they can shoot and rock out
all the lights in the street
long as I sit here alone.
The walls lean firm and big

and I hear the long trucks
slipping west out highway twenty-two
to nowhere I've ever seen
but know the land's tucked flat
and I ain't going

already been where I'm going
one man after another
I've hit enough good times
and listen, *I can stand more trouble*
than any little woman my size.

(2)   *riffin'*

They tell me to settle down
like mellow is a job
I have to retire from.
It's like they want to give me
a gold watch on a chain
a railroad watch

one I can rise and set
in & out of a dark vest pocket
rocking on a porch
thinking the track really ends
where I see the two rails pinch
long before they hit old Memphis town.
Hell, I been there, plenty.
But right here I got a woman
in a headlights-yellow blouse,
two friendly shoes that lay a shine
on every street they walk *and boy*
if I ain't riffin' tonight I hope sumthin'.

(3)   get the hell off my note

Out in the smoke of every gig I play
I pinpoint orange specks
of their cigarettes, focus on how
ice and splinters of gin
cut through fog.

I'd paint if my hand didn't shake.
Tonight is what—
the sound is what these blinks
and shapes are for
and Maxie's cornet holds

a phrase just straight enough
for me to lean in lights
and work it out
and look out Brunis
get the hell off my note.

(4)   I wouldn't be a Methodist

This morning
before it was sky
was a far child
back of the trees

79

shy in a pale green dress.
Now my kitchen's full
of yellow, yes Lord,
and the spoon fits my hand,
Jesus cares and the branches
clap along rivers of light
and *I wouldn't be a Methodist
to save me.*

the sources:

(1) Mama Yancey
(2) Louis Armstrong
(3) Pee Wee Russell
(4) Fats Waller

Early Morning Exercise,* Lake Michigan

White sands under my feet rub and crunch
and whistle against themselves. I lay their little notes
under my footprints—put them back to bed.
Like any shipwreckful of drowsiness
and breath, I can softly be taken in
by this treachery of muffled diminuendo.
Some time I'll beach myself where the music stops.

Not now. Day breaks open with gab of gulls
while dunegrass holds C-sharp above the watercrash.
I try again to discover my feet.
This rushed cacophony beating up the surf
may be the world's last jazz band shaking loose:

Listen: that clarinet is curling
green and tart its thin-lipped gripe
around hot brass that pushes it, and now
they make the sap leap up and hit the light
that plumps the blue grapes up the dunes.

*—In 1946, the National Association of Teachers of
Speech voted on the ten worst-sounding words in
English. Seven of them are: cacophony, crunch,
gripe, jazz, plump, sap, and treachery.

I Don't Like Blackberries

Someone has to beat them back:
they come out of their lazy way to sting my legs
and mouth, my rambles into summer nights.
Those little globes that huddle on their stem
could teach college math and show
the blocks in pyramids how to round and go smooth,

but the taste is the rasp of a tenor saxophone,
it honks too wide, it pumps a deeper oil
than I am ready for. My tongue would bless such shocks
after cavalry charges or in a Roman piazza,
but not right here. This is fresh and near
Lake Michigan. Our dune is in grape, more like the taste
of the Dodds clarinet on that old *Perdido Street Blues*.
So I'm starting to hack the blackberries out with the weeds
as I sickle up the leeward slope. But I think

again this May how each July my sons leap down
like riffs through the dust with purple mouths,
too young to wait for the easy unravel
of grapes on sand that will bunch up big
and blue in September frost. Once more I cut
my way around, letting them scratch and tangle and grab,
deferring one more chorus to these cool-jazz whips of juice.

(for Paul Zimmer)

Note to Marina Marquez of El Paso,
Who Sublet my Apartment for the Summer

We miss each other by just an eyelash.
We never met, and yet this place
is still your home before it drifts back home
to being mine. The shelf that's empty
of scotch keeps the smoke of tequilla,
a Flamenco album sidles up to Mahler's Eighth.
I surprised the tortillas and hot chili peppers
you left in our freezer
as I put in a bag of potatoes.

I tiptoe when thinking the hairpin under the bed.
This morning in the shower, my third day back,
through steam I noticed again
the gleam of a single dark pubic hair.
Sometimes I listen hard. At night
in the vaguely foreign country of my bed
I lie very still. I breathe it deep.
I write you nowhere, afraid you will
startle away too soon if I dare to tell you
I miss you and wish you would stay.

Wilt Dormer Going to Work

She gave him her body last night
in her king-size sheets
as a dole—to keep him, she said,
"from getting sour and hangdog."

This morning he scratches
overnight derelict whiskers,
brushes his livery breath.
Limp string between his legs, he slinks
through the yelps of the kids.
His twist of mouth
finds the scent of her forehead
sweet and he bears his steamy cup
outdoors past tree-trunks,
then whines off in low,
going to the office early.

Crisp behind glass
she is shaving cool carrots
as thin as love.

Wilt Dormer, Streaking

The long loom of curving streets
is astonished to catch his clothes
as he rips them and strews them
and runs. The dogs up Eden Drive
stop barking as though they remember
something deeper than sour bones.
"Eight o' the clock and all is well!"
he cries to startled shops
from up the graveyard wall,
and he turns out East-West Highway
into the sun, tossing his tattered
last white flags, far past surrender

past the high school now
like an old geometry problem,
bisected circle behind
with no solution at all
to the city limits of breath
where he will hide himself
in leaves
and begin the long trail back
through tree rings
past roots and berries and sheep,
arriving just before nine
at the button factory.

Wilt Dormer's Melting-Ice-Cream-Cone Sestina

Ice cream knows how to relax.
I often forget until spring
That soft can be natural.
Here comes another bird. He's blue.
If a tree forgets to change
Softly, all other colors will care.

I think I'm a child. Will the neighbors care
If I sing? They should relax,
Lick ice cream cones, change
Their shirts and blouses to spring.
Poor blue jay has to be blue—
We can change flavors. It's natural.

Maybe it's also natural
That some people no longer care
For cones. Damn. The wind just blew
This mess on my shirt. Try to relax,
Remember not to panic or spring
For phones, remember those orders to change

The pace. Let 23 flavors change
Their clothes once a week in natural
Rotation. I'll spend all spring
Being spots and runny, and never care.
I'm learning to melt and relax.
When ice cream is cold it doesn't turn blue

Unless they powdered it blue.
But why does it drip its chang-
ing down my wrist and over-relax
Into slop? Maybe the natural
Thing for ice cream is not to care.
There's something creepy and soft about spring!

Look out, that bird is naive about spring!
While I drip on the grass he sings himself blue
In the face, too childish to care.
Did that girl at the drive-in give me my change?
I don't feel really natural
Licking my hand. And, oops. Pink pill to relax.

"Take one pink pill to relax," to unwind the spring.
This tension is only natural. All right that you blew
A fuse for a change. Wash up. Try not to care.

To the Man in Room 321

You asked how it was when I got lost
from the bus and the others
and stumbled into Frazzleburg, Maryland
and tore my dress. I'm glad somebody asked.
Frazzleburg looked tired. Shredded brick houses
snarled on the edge of grumpy sidewalks.
Its hair was standing on end.
The mailman hobbled in a hemp overcoat
up and down the shocks and frowns of porches.
A rusty truck chugged alone
on an unstitched sidestreet, grinding its teeth.
But say don't I seem to remember something
didn't we live there once, me just down
the hairpin turn of Muzzle St. from you
in the white exhaust at the corner of Cock?
Why yes I think I can see you now
ripping the sacks of gorse and furze and fratch
with sharp fingernails. You were bigger then.
Was that you? Was that me? I see
why you asked about my trip, it's nice
to relive those good old days that fade away.

X

Teacher's mark for a mistake,
X signs our teenage letters with a kiss,
then waits for us in gunsights up the road.

X is the sign all make who cannot make
their names, the picture children may not see,

the train which just might strike train Y
if we fail to solve the time for its space.

Turn your X in the air and bless yourself:
someone is marking a map in a rented room.
X is the stranger. Unknown quantity. Spy.
A half-wild light ray child-in-a-manger
shape to which we nail our fears.

Crossroad, crisis, crux, X is outrageous
crucifix brought bloody in through gates.

Sometimes when speech breaks down, we let
X mark the spot where our bombs will rain

Or X is the little grave we won't forgive.
We drop to our knees in rage or worship. Come to X.

(for L.P.)

VI

Incarnality

Meditation on my old Bike

The frame was a harp swung low and blue
and I could ride it higher than Psalm Nineteen.
The silver fenders would lay the mud back down
on the road like hands that made a blessing
and leap the light right past my eyes
while green & white streamers twisted from grips
like wintergreen candy hair of angels alight.
Just under the round sweet ache of legs
that made it go, my feet could ride the singing choir
of coasters somehow tradenamed *New Departure*,
hinting I could anytime lift clean off the street
and into an Ascension. I never rose. The left foot
always held back to the faithless brake and gave me
the little broken song of sanctity, the benediction
to holy blacktop, sprocket, wind, oil, chain.

Holding On

Words like *holy ghost* and *clair du lune* and *gone*
meant the two violins asleep on our old upright Moser.
Snowlight through the grillwork of curtains.
The chain damper-control in the hall was shut
so I couldn't hear the furnace breathe. Sometimes
a truck in passing ached three strings together,
all in tune. In the dark of my family's sleep
I wondered where *Liebestraum's* notes could be
curled up in the stillness, with all the fires banked.

I almost like goodbyes. I'm never afraid
of those shadows of valleys you close behind your eyes.
Alone I stretch toward sleep along the longest wind
the shore can play; I think about breath and drift,
and more about coming back—and even more

about holding on. Whatever it is that blows
those tulips up through blow-pipe stems into balloons
doesn't let them fly. Birds don't get lighter
and rise as they loose the weight
of their whistling up the unwashed air.
Come morning I'll watch a swallow dive
down the cries and branches to my
water-logged broken fence, where it's
heavy enough again to sing the silence you leave.

Fresh Fruit for Breakfast

All night we were softly tangled in the sky's
vineyard of small white grapes

now that much more than the seven flavors of Jello
shake their covers from orchards and hills

o let the children's wild shouts upstairs
steal our dark thunder of hallelujahs

let fruitstains on their mouths be psalms
kissing hello the seventy thousand tons of light

that fleshed the dark this year, rejoicing
in juice of these berries, peaches, plums.

The Early Morning Women in the Rue des Fleurs

spill over fences fat
or bulge from blue window boxes

jostle in crooked lines
with yellow shopping baskets

spring red from cracks
or purple and bunch at corners

while up the light
the pink & white behind glass

shine like maidens high and lean
white and pink.

(for Sibbie O'Sullivan)

Distances

(Christmas, 1973)

"The Kahoutec Comet right now,"
he whispered, "is only
seventy million miles from the sun.
Pass the word. Repent."
His wilderness eyes,
holding subway lights,
watched my reflection in the window of the train
as though I were
electrons from space.
NINEVAH REPENT, his tract began—
pale man hanging
to the rib of a train by a strap.

I know how an end can come
more likely in a flash of Buick
at noon, on the corner nearest home—
a shower of glass near a landmark tree.
Destruction is inches, like love.

Surfaced again and unrepentant
I walk the charted blocks
under streetlights over snow.
I pace the city star by star.
I know how long a mile can go on.
Maybe God knows too
who repented once softly
this time of year
slipping down light-years
with another disrupting star,
but the prophet down in the subway
watches still
darkly through the window
for his stop.

Ways to Measure

Weigh raindrops in the fall
and you can feel
the speed at which the cold is coming in.

The absence of the son who died
grows tall in the doorway
where he had them mark his eighteen years
inch by inch.

A measure for decorum:
as restrained as the lunatic cabbage,
which opens only to moonlight.

Her anger one night was two cups
of gin. He got the moon
down to just the size of his fist.

A student said about a poem by Hardy,
"I wonder why he called it a lonely house.
There seems to be
at least one other person living there."

A Double Contention Against the Scriptures

I don't understand how the old lament
There is no new thing under the sun
can be true. I see
new things. A schoolgirl showed me
a painting she made today

and now I have this picture
in my head, surely it's new,
of ghosts as wavey lines of light
that try to thicken to colors

so they can form and come back.
The girl said dew is the tears
the dead people leave on the grass
when they can't quite make it home.

That's new. So is the thought I got
that now every stir
of shadow through air
craves having a body

and these things ache alive
like the newly closing space
left by your son
I try to forget

who died last week. I remember
Let not the sun go down upon thy wrath
but tonight that miser
same old penny sun
slid down again red on my wrath.

(for the parents of Gus)

Touching It

(1)

Snow

I have drowsed in and out of four naps.
The first snow, falling all day outside,
makes fur of any good room.
While in dreams I was trying to find
four little things I had lost,
the snow was piling high
and drifting the sills, the road.
Swirls of woolgathered white:
I close my eyes and shake, and down it comes.

It covers anything. I have forgotten
all but the shapes
of lost things in the dreams.
The late-summer death of my son
gets deep and in place, like the car
out there on the road, drifting in snow.

(2)

Glass

I found beach sand in a pocket
this coldest day of the winter—
he would have liked those pulverized
stars, rising from valleys
inside the jeans
and reflecting a hot
light bulb in the closet.

But he would throw the stars away
as I just did,
brushing them off.

What are you going to be
when you grow up
I ask my aging face in the glass.
I always ask, but with the tap
I make quick clouds of steam,
the crystal ball is clouded,
no answer but a wink and a young
cocked grin which fogs over.

(3)

Walk

This broken stone
says I'll get my finger on you
so gently
you'll stir up and kick with me through sand
like a friend

mortal and afraid
surprised to have someone along
as cool as you
you shivering old bastard
death.

(4)

Survivor

My youngest son has put in his cap
the good stones,
the ones he believes in.
He is out in the breakers.

I bow down before stone:
a glazed one ordains me
to be its thin streak
of red mouth.

I'm an old stone. Cool.
The spark is in deep.
Now I can start to talk
to the tips of his fingers.

(1974)

First Climb up Three Surfers' Peak

(a dune at Lost Valley, on Lake Michigan,
named in memory of John Jellema, Todd Eaddy,
and Bill Smalligan—d. 1973)

"Tell the vision to no man." (Matt. 17, 9)

After we drove three stakes and nailed
the wooden sign *Three Surfers' Peak*
into its foot, I climbed
the dune, stood up to
its wind on the razorback edge
to watch and wait.
                    No sign.
No countenance shone upon me.
I could not get blinded by light
of the sand and surf.
Although the waves and the beach
got small, there was no Transfiguration.
The three memorial boys didn't show,
nothing did, although
I swore to god
I would have left them once again
and come back down
from that forbidden place
to hunks and beating colors,
watercrash, the timid dartings of deer
into long grass, cry of a child
and all the empty corners—back to
these tangled things they knew.
I swore like Jesus
I'd work back down to love
and the faces in streets,
but I knew this note I was leaving

could be the lie
on which to twist my way up
to the light
an hour before I climbed the peak
so no one would know what happened
just in case it did.

The Self Trying to Leave the Body that it is

You're all skin the rough heat of sumac
thickened with bruises. Body, you pant
rank steam while onions eat our breath.
You're itch, you're a grind of sockets,
you're meat that sags and jerks in turn.
Why do I think of sour cabbage clubbed
purple and drying in halls? Don't answer:
if I let you speak for yourself
you'll chug and saw like oldtime Sunday
in a wooden church, all maroon and black,
far from the yellow mercy of blowing wheat.
You want me under your skin—I want

to fly light and not remember pull, wing.
Just go away. Go knock me some possible
door through your cells. I'll rise
some hollow way. Out distant fields
I yearn to see the brassy fat bells
stretch thin into harpstrings, hairs,
auras, until they pale into strands
of wind over snowfields, whispers of cold.
Old lover, drag and heft, why can't you
let me break out? Take heart: I've crossed
our arms like this over our chest so we
can separate in the dignity of a sign.

Just Breathe

You and that coming breath
have been through thin together.
It arrives with its little hands
full of drift and absence
toward something like home.
A shutter claps in the wind.
Beneath the beats of the heart
that murmur *be* and *be*,
air takes the shape of a wing
and every thing catches its weight.

Just breathe. In and out.
The next wave startles the next:
the snow will rearrange
its drifts along the fence,
sailcloth will belly and luff
as the breeze swings to the south.
Anything else that's part
of the rhythm will follow:
breathe again, loosen, dip,
lean on the dancing.

Beyond where breath disappears
far over your shoulder, stars
refuse to take note, they go only
out and out. But never mind.
Everything sings to a gentle
raising and drawing of blinds
and a turning up and down of lights.
For all its domesticity,
the next breath is the wildest
rumor of angels you know.

VII

The Eighth Day

On Course

The first two tacks were a wide zig-zag
that set me deep in this grey and abstract
compass-point where the wind is coming from.
West-by-southwest. I'm so far out from where
the sandbar trips the water into my dark Third Coast

that I can't make out in the rumple of dunes behind me
Three Surfers' Peak, that landmark for Lost Valley—
the one name we've ever found for home. The first tack
took me south; the second stretched longer west. Before
the final third of the journey I pause, point up the wind,

let the sails luff. The old contention is done.
I need some Michigan treeline in my eye. I turn.
The sail snaps full and jerks the little boat,
the prow swings to and starts to dive and run.
I re-rig the tackle light

because now I own the wind I have put behind me,
go where it blows, and it blows a straight course
to a touchable distance northeast, to fire
and some supper, let's say, red splotch of cottage
on the thin string of beach. I bind to the cleat

the tugging lines, then float my hands adrift;
as if in sleep I lift the daggerboard out
and let myself plane like a sudden surfer
exploding out of the grey into blue and white.
So this is the run that being lost was for.

Married to nothing but weather, I lean back
with the waking tiller and try to map out
the old high ways of stars I will not need
that fall unseen through the afternoon blaze of sky.
When I touch the breakers ahead,

the wind will pass me along from the surge
of one whitecap to the splash
of the next, the next, the next. I ride
that easy heartbeat all the way home.

On Edge

Be grateful to the gunman
Who inches the shade aside
to pin you on the fine lines
of his cross. Give thanks to the wild
night of dogs gone mad, or rising ice,
thanks to the drunk who weaves
his bleary headlights cold across
the hairs on the back of your neck.
Bless the man's knuckles that whiten around
a length of pipe, empty freightcars standing
in snow, bless light from the mortuary.
Hum in the dark to the halting
knock of your heart on the door of its cave,
sing praise to the loss
of grip underneath as you skid.

You're learning the edge.
This crisp morning you walk old shoes
with the grace of a child skipping
in summer. The tips of your fingers
retain the touch of the skin
on the ears of your sons.
And even it it rains, just let it rain:
still you will sprinkle your lawn
tonight in the dark.

Skating it Off

On blustery days, iced in,
I lash up the biting thongs
of ancestral wooden skates.
I lean into cheering winds
down old Frisian canals,
hands behind my back,
determined to show her.
But I have no cap or scarf
to brighten the streaming air,
I always shiver and swerve
and almost blow off the margin
and then the thin page cracks
and I splash through.

This time I'm going
to win the silver skates.
Watch: red tile roofs
under which we won't live
sail past while the bare arms
of only windmills wave
and I glide like butter
from stroke to long stroke,
leaving alternate wakes
of Delft-blue sparks
smoking high in the elms
behind, all the way into
the lights of Dokkum

before I notice that no one
is watching, she is not there.

Dawn Train through Valparaiso

The year the Civil War turned back to sleep,
some Latinate dream of Paradise Valley stirred
here in Indiana, lost amid alien corn.
In the mercy of dark I can turn this Valparaiso into
the one in Chile, where I have never been: tangled flowers
up mountainside suburbs and over those Andes
the way Neruda once fled, an outlaw with a disguised
bundle of poems and two good bottles of wine.
But in these streets, in the flashing light of Blatz, Blatz,
no one will hunt you down for subverting the system
with poems. They will never take notice. Here they make
tankcars full of paint and Lutheran college degrees.
Dante makes pizza. The truckers from Gary
and Chi call this place Valpo, plain as motor oil.
The downtown houses are teeth in rusty gears.

In the dark train window I try to remember my face
fifteen years before this passing through: lecturer
with a breaking life who came to Valpo U. like a truck to pronounce
the end of Christian Humanism. Weak research but right
perception, that untyped conference paper lies still
with half my life in a box marked "to be filed." I know again,
clean through my dusty face to the squeal of signal lights,
that "four hundred years of humanist faith in man
leave us longing for half-remembered places, for miraculous rain."

Here comes the light. Indiana has nowhere to hide.
It didn't really have the time to nurture a cathedral
out of these broken plains. What is missing is not
the skyward shot that's dizzy swaying off the tips
of spires, what we ache for is the weight
of hewn stone holding down here, grave
with us through glare or night, silent
yet huge with mass to wait with us
for some end that could bring us round.

The train is running out of town
to mourn. It picks up speed.
Far on the edge, in an old frame house,
a muffled light in an upstairs room
says someone is sick, or dying.
We are hurtling past someone's end,
no one knows how to stop,
get off this train. God's priest for now,
obsolete as the pre-dawn train for Chicago
that no longer stops, I mumble remotely
the Latin I never learned: *pace, misere,*
mea maxima culpa. I make Christ's furious sign
with a fist where the dinning bell
tears open red in the dark near the end
at the dangerous crossing.

Going to Work at Yaddo

At the artists' colony
I leave the mansion
and walk to work
across frozen grass
in old shoes and jacket.
I see through breath
the hard stones.
Dark pines are watching.
Thermos under my arm,
I swagger,
swing the black lunchpail,
emblem of manhood,
whistle each day
different tunes
from the thirties.

Child awakened
by factory whistle
I watch
through cold glass
a whistling man
stride off to work.
Just before
his key makes touch
with the

studio door
he looks about
the empty woods.
I am not there.

Crab Cactus

Deformed and staunched like the stump
of a claw, it hunches toward light.
The stalk that it is accumulates
its fleshy lack of decency
time out of mind in the sands.

Eons ago it sulked itself pale
and fled the cool shadows of Eden,
sure that the spoken *it is good*
of Genesis could not apply.
Now an old exile and hardly
a plant, it sucks the air
like a stone and does not cry out.

But late each December for just one night
it forgets the feud. Mad as a magus
it brings between spikes one bloom
of outcast star, God only knows
to whom from where or why.

(after the Frisian of Fedde Schurer, 1898-1968)

116

Letter from Home

At the Annapolis docks the yawl *Blue Puffin*
is for sale. So is the rough old skipjack
Grey Ghost. I buy

a plastic cup of worms,
drive Highway 2 five miles,
turn down that two-track road
trespassing past the signs that say I must not
to fish for perch. The point is

white sand below high pines
that cleaves Round Bay.
Since you and I took a wrong turn

blind into its lights, the point is
ours. Still
you haunt the plink
a sinker makes. And if you claim
what can't be bought

and forgive such roads the map won't tell—
then some time at that point
or if not then or there
in the twinkling of an eye
I'll see you, trespasser.

(to son John, 1970; revised 7/31/73)

117

The Weather is Always Good

Changes of weather curl inside
and wait to resound. Sometimes
grief stretches out in our eyes,
lies tight and thickens the tissue
until the lights coming in are dim.
Its wind is black and still.
And even this is seasoning, fresh

and right until curtains flutter inward
and grief plays light
through trembling poplars, light
in a net of mist on the lake
that we watch thoughtless and mute.
From the stir of internal murmur we say
how impossibly bright these things are.

(After a Macedonian poem by Aĉo Ŝopov)

White on White

Just in from the snow, my mind
is the white road out there
filling in as it died behind me
all the way home. Perhaps
as it lost its way in and out
it ran out of one kind of time.

I shake and brush my coat
and lashes and stomp my feet
but something is not going to leave.
The white star lights
I may once have steered by
still fall down streets
and lawns and down behind my eyes,
down optic caves, like galaxies
receding into a rim of space.
White has followed me home from the snow.

I listen here behind the door in the dark:
nothing up the sky is so far out
that its soundings cannot resonate
the stillest mind: and now I know deep
that the white in my yard is not still:
its mass is energy, it lies
like the black holes implicit for years
in Einstein's abstract equation
lying there quiet on paper. I hold on
tight along an icy curve of thought:

That there's some eighth day of the week
inside the window reflection that jumps
into place as I flick on the light: there
for a second my brown coat is raining, my hood
is still tied, the monk I was is humming soft
as candleflame to a white figure rising from white.

119

Waving

When they propped my Grandma high up
in the oxygen tent, she started
to bob just slightly up and down, up
and down. She nodded and smiled
through the plastic window,
then blushing in white she waved from
the sleek little one-horse cutter
her dapper young Frisian-
American husband just bought, waved
to us through blue-tint isinglass
as she clipped down the immigrant streets
of southside Chicago sixty years before
her astonished grandson stood there,
coached by an uncle, and waved goodbye.

Letter from Friesland to my Sons

Fear burns its lights late in America's night
    and I'm not there. Up here in Friesland
learning to read the surviving sounds our ancestors made,
    I have cut the electric din of English.
It is like a vow of silence. Deprived of the insight of speech,
    I only hear as echo some far
and ancient music. Forgive me. I have chosen for now to be dumb.

This flat land I try to claim is a tiny forever;
    the four towns I can name through my window
are only the middle distance—the eye goes on and on
    swimming the slow flow of canals.
The cobbled roads, unimpeded by hills, graze slowly as sorrow
    beside the still water that always returns.
The seasons stay, they doze lightly as ages beneath each other—

there are no junctures, time circulates like a heaviness
    in speech, like village smiles, like sun
and nitrates churning through cows and grass. A seamless world.
    So I think I remember from centuries ago
these Frisian faces, and I know I've heard before tonight

this stormy wind, the thumps and shouts of an angry preacher
    wing collar askew as he breaks
his diphthongs against indifferent roofs and branches and stars.
    And the calm is familiar, too: the way
consonants soften and wash like tides, and never tick.

Adrift like a child drowsy in church who wants to make
    a world in the smell of his mother's fur,
I try to make from this beginning, before the end
    of our sweet good time on the earth, just once,
images that turn on themselves and echo ahead, out of time.
    Mute but only partially deaf,
I write notes for now on the third side of the page.

121

I'll come back, of course, but back each time some small part short
of the whole way back to where you grow.
So listen: old Frisians say what to do about mystery and loss,
about all the unspeakable beauty and grief:
if it can't be said, a Dokkum proverb goes, *then you must sing it.*
I'm learning. Forgive me. I want to have words
with you tonight, but the canal going back has no translation.

With the American Wind Symphony, Crossing Lake Ontario at Night

How can a symphony orchestra, touring by boat,
work its poet-in-residence? Virgil Thomson says poets
are pre-historic whales who still spout from habit.
I feel like that. So this noon I made the pot of stew.
But if poets can still write something suspended, like music. . . .
If the wheel were mine tonight, the log would start in D-minor
with seagulls. No reason why. Something like this:

Deep behind sunset the seagulls rest along shore
at Ontario Place. They burn asleep
near orange pavilions in darkness,
heavy with plastic french fries and catsup.
If they remember a thrill in the wing from diving
these breakers for perch, their fat dreams of it dim
like the lights of Toronto shrinking behind the wake.

Shocks of moonlight touch the waves like wands
off starboard. I am eating a goat heart sandwich
now thirty miles from any shore. There are flies.
Will flies be out here when men are not?
Can they rest on water after the last boat
has left? Now there are no lights from towns
or farms. The engine skips a throb

to our darkened pilot house glowing red
and the ice in my whiskey is gone. Because
no natural predator hunts this awful inland sea, I scan
the American shore for danger and wonder how far out
we are now, what key, how deep we are as I raise my collar
about my throat and decide there's something here
to catch that the logbooks will not report.

(for Robert Boudreau)

Even Pigeons

Alright. Just for a glance at a time
the philosopher Berkeley is right.
Look how the drizzle
holds Michigan porchlights
here
    in Manhattan
where no street exists
till a window shade
or a taxi or even pigeons
start up from the shadow
of a hill that isn't there.

Meditation on Coming Out of a Matinee

I try to trust the light
before I step off into it.
I think death is not dark,
I know my fear of the light.
Death is more light than I can think.

I've seen what death feels like:
I woke one morning to light from
beyond the white curtain
but the lamps in the room still on
bright as if it's already night.

Yes, like that.

Letter to Myra Sklarew, Visiting Mekounida, on the Island of Evvoia, in Greece

Lost Valley
Montague, Michigan
7 July, 1982

Dear Myra, in one of the fifteen houses of that high village
you need: by now you would join the lamentation
of ancient women sighing dark as shawls
to think I had sent the postman and his donkey
struggling up that dusty mountain path
from the little harbor at Karystos all the way up
only to say *how are you I am fine we miss you here.*

This must be worth his hire. I pray to God the ding
of goatbells and a closer hum of bees in thyme
will make light of the road this note must go.
I pray for the donkey's feet, for three faithful hands
at least that will cross the postman a blessing,
for cold water up the way that tastes of stone,
for a breeze and a hush of wine back down to Karystos.

And now it feels so ancient and good to pray aloud
like a peasant I also pray for rain to lay quick hands
on dust, for the strong green breath of onions in high fields.
Peace to the sheep who graze in rocks. May olive trees
push thick and heavy up the tilted yards and groves,
let lutes tonight and sleep twine deep as candlelight
in vines, Lord make the cheese turn gently in the crocks.

From the Great Lakes I have only small news: our swamp that went
almost dry behind the dune is back this year. Down here
the bullfrogs snap their banjo strings all night, and crickets twitch.
Machines knocked down the oldest house in town, the blacksmith's sh
We're meeting in the small white church to try to stop the bomb.
At dawn just after a storm, near the shore, I saw a scarlet tanager
ignite black pine—this highpriest without camouflage who still

126

survives in light. But what I must tell you most: I saw
the way light leans into the greenstain side of a shipwrecked beam
and it made me feel something about the weather
of which a nervous laugh is only a modern translation.
The moon had been eclipsed, there had been that storm, and then
this other light, this almost microscopic whelming. Something is wrong.
Tell me if you feel the trembling there above Karystos. Love.

The Eighth Day:New and Selected Poems, Rod Jellema's third book of poems, shapes and unifies the major motifs of his work up to now by relocating many of the poems from *Something Tugging the Line* (1974) and *The Lost Faces* (1979) among the newer poems. The work hailed as "bursting with raw poetic talent" (*Library Journal*) ten years ago is now rich in breadth, exploring with both pathos and comedy "the stabs of joy that leap from deep inside a fallen world of redeemed, incarnate things."

Rod Jellema was born in Holland, Michigan, and studied at Calvin College and at the University of Edinburgh (Scotland). He is director of the creative writing program at the University of Maryland, where he has taught literature since 1955. For more than fifteen years, he has been publishing poems regularly, about 200 in such magazines as *Poetry Northwest, Field, Poetry Now, Poet Lore,* and *The Georgia Review*. His awards include a Discovery Grant (1970) from the National Endowment for the Arts and a National Endowment Fellowship (1980), and "mainly, a long shelf of solid books of poems by former students."